A Huge Hog Is a BIG PIG

a rhyming word game

Francis McCall & Patricia Keeler

GREENWILLOW BOOKS · *An Imprint of HarperCollinsPublishers*

For Maureen and Molly,
who taught us how to play Stinky Pinky,
and Grace, Gera, and Hayden,
who showed us how the game would look.
We love you guys!

— F. M. and P. K.

Many thanks to Daniel Fisher, Briyana Fisher, Samantha Alicandri, Samantha Kluepfel,
John Kluepfel, Rachel Wunder, Lynette Collazo, Allan Takeshita, Saskia Salak, Tonya Ramos,
Alan Watson, Alexandra Kardian, Hayden Williams, Chandler Price, Courtney Orvig, Shawn McCall,
Zahyria Temple, Emily Trent, Allison Whitmore, John-Michael Rollins, Lindsey Space, Hunter Space,
Isaiah Cruz, Elontae Terry, Anthony Woodson, Adam Bowers, Almee Jane Gamboa, Elijah Coggins,
Stone Coggins, Jack Coggins, Siena Dellafave, Dylan Fitzsimmons, Silas Emerson, Perry Continente,
Dana McCall, Hayley McCall, Ted McCall, Dottie Martin, Vince Sharp, Rana Ranch Bullfrog Farm,
Custom Parrot Network, Kathleen McKee, Marilyn McKee, Bluebird Gap Farm, Maymont Foundation,
Space Farms Zoo & Museum, The Pet Company, Companion Animal Placement, and Emerson Dairy.

A Huge Hog Is a Big Pig: A Rhyming Word Game
Copyright © 2002 by Francis McCall and Patricia Keeler
All rights reserved.
Printed in Hong Kong by South China Printing Company (1988) Ltd.
www.harperchildrens.com

The full-color photographs were reproduced from 35-mm Kodachrome slides.
The text type is Opti Acton.

 Library of Congress Cataloging-in-Publication Data
McCall, Francis X.
A huge hog is a big pig: a rhyming word game / by Francis McCall and Patricia Keeler.
   p.   cm.
"Greenwillow Books."
Summary: A variety of mostly farm animals are introduced with such phrases
as a granny nanny, a soggy doggy, and a loose goose.
ISBN 0-06-029765-4 (trade). ISBN 0-06-029766-2 (lib. bdg.)
1. Animals—Juvenile fiction. [1. Animals—Fiction.] I. Keeler, Patricia A. II. Title.
PZ10.3.M125 Hu 2002   [E]—dc21   2001016153

10 9 8 7 6 5 4 3 2 1 First Edition

A huge hog is a...

BIG PIG.

A swamp croaker is a...

BOG FROG.

A chatty parrot is a...

WORDY BIRDIE.

A wet hound is a...

SOGGY DOGGY.

A chubby kitty is a...

FAT CAT.

A silly rabbit is a...

FUNNY BUNNY.

A chicken coop is a...

HEN DEN.

A grandmother goat is a...

GRANNY NANNY.

Cattle food is...

COW CHOW.

A runaway gander is a ...

LOOSE GOOSE.

A cozy beetle is a...

SNUG BUG.

A fidgety gobbler is a...

JERKY
TURKEY.

QUACK PACK.

A puppy kiss is a...

POOCH SMOOCH.

A happy father is a...

GLAD DAD.